7 Critical Mistakes Employees Make in a Downsizing

Power Moves to Survive the "New Working Model"

Michael Sanders MA, PMP

Copyright © 2014 Michael Sanders

All rights reserved.

ISBN-13: 978-1502997166
ISBN-10: 1502997169

DEDICATION

To all my brave friends who refused to be victims of the *New Working Model.*

This page intentionally left blank.

CONTENTS

	Preface	vii
1	Welcome to the Land of Oz	1
2	The Seven Critical Mistakes	5
3	Mistake 1 - Resisting Change	9
4	Mistake 2 - Feeling Like a Victim	11
5	Mistake 3 - Playing New Game by Old Rules	13
6	Mistake 4 - Controlling the Uncontrollable	15
7	Mistake 5 - Slowing Down	17
8	Mistake 6 - Psychologically Unplug	19
9	Mistake 7 - Avoiding New Assignments	21
10	Eight Power Moves to Thrive in Chaos	23
11	Survival Syndrome	29
12	Challenge of the New Working Model	37
	Templates, Exercises, Systems	45
	References and Suggested Reading	51
	Seminars	55
	Free Downloads	56

This page intentionally left blank.

PREFACE

I thought I could do anything.

Growing up on the other side of the tracks, in trailer parks, poor and on welfare, you survived only if you were tough – and if not tough, appearing tough. Winning and money were the ultimate judges of success in that world. Years later when I entered the workforce, I respected only toughness, winning, high salaries, and status. And boy did I win. And I was compelled to win every single battle, most of my own making.

Good grief, these organizations did not know what to do with me. Every disagreement I entered into was a dogfight with everything on the line. From my standpoint, winner takes all. Although I was considered very competent in my job, I was not really trusted by my management or my co-workers due to the caustic nature of my wins. Being able to think and argue effectively on my feet and having no stops, I was usually able to win my many confrontations. However, over time these wins were detrimental to my organization, my teams, and me. So when things eventually got messy, and they always did, I simply found another job. Most of the time with a raise in pay! My self-centered logic told me if I made more money, I was right. So I won. Right?

Then one day, years later and after a sea of job changes and failed business relationships, I sat in my car in the parking lot of a department store and broke down. I began crying uncontrollably and did not know why. After a few minutes, I saw my entire past unfold in front of me. I saw all the people I had hurt, all the organizational damage done, and all the squandered opportunities given to me, but thrown away for ridiculously small gains. All of my wins were in the name of my own power in a command and control business world. I saw the complete fallacy of my accomplishments and of my work ethic.

On that day, I promised myself I would change. My new mission would be to make a positive impact in whatever organization I worked in and in the world. But to do this, I needed to re-educate myself, I needed to learn and practice a better way to work with those reporting to me, my co-workers, and my management.

Eight years later, I had completed an anger management program; two Organizational Management degrees; facilitated numerous workshops in Native American practices; and presented management topics at over 150 corporations, universities and companies. Topics included organizational management, organizational psychology, advanced communications, and emotional intelligence. I even wrote a white paper for the Project Management Institute and a book on advanced management. But something was still missing. Downsizing.

I realized my passion was to find out how to empower the average worker in a positive way – in contrast to my desperate attempt earlier in life to empower myself through self-centered intimidation and winning at all costs.

The *7 Critical Mistakes Employees Make in a Downsizing* describes the nature of "victims" as opposed to successful and empowered workers in the typical dysfunctional organization.

These empowered workers use tactics quite different than the "win-at-all-costs" practices I used as a young man or assumption of the "victim" paradigm acquired by so many. Empowered employees skillfully divert winning to their teams, groups and organizations, rather than to themselves. And they do this while continuing with their own development. These individuals actually fuel and drive organizations and, in fact, need little management.

It is ironical that empowered employees distinguish themselves in organizations by dissolving into them. They win through the successes of their teams, workgroups, and companies using competence, not overachievement.

These next-generation workers power their organizations by accepting complete accountability for themselves, their work groups, education, experience, skillsets, relationships, and personal growth – everything around them. They assume the posture of empowerment rather than waiting for it to be bestowed. And they innovate as *intrapreneurs*, or entrepreneurs "within" companies, to do the unimaginable – make something out of nothing.

I believe this new empowered worker is the future of successful organizations in this millennium. These workers will ride the downsizing wave rather than fall victim to it. The key attributes of this new type of worker includes self-empowerment, respect of their peers, trust from their management, expertise in their fields, higher education, valued skills, passion in their work, and accountability. These workers will also eventually replace management as we know it – needing none.

This book shows us how we can become empowered and highly valued in the seeming chaos of downsizing. And although we may not dodge the downsizing bullet in every case, we can use downsizing energy to ride its wave, to thrive.

By the way, after observing, researching, and applying techniques for organizational survival for over 10 years, I need to add one more thought in your organizational navigation basket. There is a good possibility that when an organization begins its downsizing trek, years of reductions, reorganizations, mergers and buyouts may follow. So you need to consider whether you really want a future at the very company you are holding onto for dear life. That said, every single technique discussed in this book still applies. If for nothing more than getting you ready for the next, more prominent phase of your career.

Best to you. Mike.

ACT III, SCENE I -ENTER HAMLET

To be, or not to be, that is the question - whether 'tis nobler in the mind to suffer the slings and arrows of outrageous fortune, or to take arms against a sea of troubles, and by opposing end them?

To die, to sleep - no more; and by a sleep, to say we end the heartache, and the thousand natural shocks that flesh is heir to?

'Tis a consummation devoutly to be wished. To die, to sleep, to sleep, perchance to dream; aye, there's the rub, for in that sleep of death, what dreams may come, when we have shuffled off this mortal coil, must give us pause.

There's the respect that makes calamity of so long life: For who would bear the whips and scorns of time, the oppressor's wrong, the proud man's contumely, the pangs of despised love, the law's delay, the insolence of office, and the spurns that patient merit of the unworthy takes, when he himself might his quietus make with a bare bodkin?

Who would fardels bear, to grunt and sweat under a weary life, but that the dread of something after death, the undiscovered country, from whose bourn no traveler returns, puzzles the will, and makes us rather bear those ills we have, than fly to others that we know not of.

Thus conscience does make cowards of us all, and thus the native hue of resolution is sicklied o'er, with the pale cast of thought, And enterprises of great pitch and moment, with this regard their currents turn awry and lose the name of action.

Soft you now, the fair Ophelia?

Nymph, in thy orisons be all my sins remembered.

(Kittredge,1939)

This page intentional left blank.

1

WELCOME TO THE LAND OF OZ
THE PROMISE OF THE NEW WORKING MODEL

Excuse me, can we postpone the executions?

I have been through seven downsizings in my career. Also referred to as layoffs, reductions-in-force, rightsizings, organizational changes, their result was always the same. Good people lost their jobs questionably with questionable results. In viewing the process each time, I became fascinated with the selection (or should I say de-selection) criteria, the organizational structures produced to handle the same business with a smaller workforce, the short-term consequences of the loss, and long-term results affecting the business' products, goodwill, and culture.

> So many get caught up in the process ...

To learn more, I went back to school to study organizations. Eventually I earned a Master's degree in organizational management with a focus in organizational change and leadership. In my graduate studies, I researched and wrote extensively about downsizing preconditions, psychology, processes and after-effects.

As it turned out, most of the downsizings I experienced produced one of two results: the company either went out of business or eventually hired back the workforce it disposed of. These results were actually quite predictable. The re-acquired workforces were usually more expensive, less qualified and marginally effective in the long term. No lasting good came from these downsizings, and the companies that survived did so at great cost and even greater loss.

So why do I bring this up?

It might surprise you to know the rationale, strategy and long-term effects of a downsizing have little or nothing to do with those downsized in the end. The purpose of this book is to address this concept and give those in perceived harm's way some strategies, skills and tools to do well, very well.

So many employees experiencing potential job loss in a downsizing get caught up in its justification, the threat and the downsizing process. They invest herculean attention and effort in complaining, attempting to understand why, and even trying to change the course of the downsizing itself. This ends up being little more than wasted energy and lost time. This lost energy and time would be much better spent using the ideas and tactics presented in the following chapters.

What follows is an understandable and practical look at downsizing and seven critical mistakes employees make before, during and after the process is complete (although I have to tell you the process is rarely ever complete.). No matter what your management may tell you, one downsizing usually leads to another.

The seven critical mistakes employees make in a downsizing can lead to the exact opposite of the intended results: job loss, loss of position, loss of salary, loss of a discernable future. But these mistakes can be reversed. The empowering and practical concepts presented in this book counteract the potential negative effects of downsizing and strengthen employee value, development, organizational smarts, and physical health. They also nurture happiness along the way.

This page intentional left blank.

2

THE 7 CRITICAL MISTAKES

Here it comes.

It seems organizational downsizings are becoming more the common occurrence rather than the exception in the new global economy. As a downsizing approaches and settles in, the *New Working Model* presented by the new organizational leadership may present formidable challenges for employees to perform at high levels as well as enjoy their work.

Most of us fear downsizings because of their potential negative effects on our lives. After all, we could lose our jobs or be placed into jobs we don't really like! And job loss could mean not only a loss of income, but a loss of benefits, social connections and self-esteem as well.

> ... the New Working Model ...

These fears are not without merit. If we lost our job, we might not be able to find another one right away. There is not only the lead time of job hunting but the stigma of finding work while you're jobless. If we cannot find a new job soon enough, we might need to dip into our precious savings. What if our savings were not enough to cover the unemployment period? We may end up losing everything or embarrassingly have to ask our family or friends for help. But even if we had enough savings, we would still be compelled, as responsible adults, to downsize our lifestyles into something much less than we have right now. Our lives would change, downward.

Additionally, if we lost our job, we could also lose the benefits we may take for granted right now such as medical, dental, vision and life insurance. Our 401K plan, pension plan, educational reimbursement, and profit sharing may be on hold.

There are so many benefits that could be lost or impaired if we lost our jobs.

There is also the social cost of job loss. We may lose touch with friends and co-workers. Or subsist at home in the potentially humiliating role of the unemployed, anxious to find a new work while swimming in a sea of other qualified job hunters.

What follows is a discussion of seven critical mistakes employees make in a downsizing with this very real possibility of losing their jobs. Each of these typical errors in action and inaction is followed by a prescription on how to avoid and correct the error. The seven mistakes are:

1. Resisting change
2. Feeling like a victim
3. Playing the new game by the old rules
4. Trying to control the uncontrollable
5. Slowing down
6. Psychologically unplugging
7. Avoiding new assignments

All seven downsizing mistakes can be neutralized and even reversed with a bit of tactical and strategic thinking, coupled with a positive attitude. The prescriptions that follow the descriptions of mistakes can help position you not only to survive, but actually thrive in the seemingly chaotic environment of the downsizing's *New Working Model*.

Following the descriptions and remedies for the seven critical downsizing mistakes, eight power moves are presented to add a solid foundation and strength to your downsizing navigation. These power moves include:

1. Exercising
2. Drinking more water
3. Having fun, smiling and laughing
4. Getting plenty of sleep
5. Being grateful
6. Saying nice things to yourself
7. Simplifying your life
8. Forgiving and forgetting

In the end, these remedies may not save your job, but they will certainly give you a fighting chance in the seeming chaos of the downsizing process. At a minimum, they will put you in a superior position in the marketplace if you need to find new employment.

The ultimate goal here is to become your own "Superhero" and ride the downsizing wave and thrive rather than go under or simply survive. The key to winning this battle is simple. "Refuse to be a victim."

3

MISTAKE 1
RESISTING CHANGE

Champion change.

Change is the main ingredient and requirement in the downsizing recipe book. From an organizational point of view, change is required to survive and is here to stay. As pointed out by Harvard professor David Garvin (Garvin, et al, 2004), successful organizations of the future will not only need to change, but change rapidly. It follows that the workforces in these successful organizations will also need to change rapidly as well.

Rather than resisting change, make a few quick adjustments and develop the habit of "instant alignment." That is, "respond to" change immediately and consistently by grabbing on and even *championing* change.

> **... develop the habit of instant alignment ...**

Making the decision to not only change, but to change quickly reduces stress and helps you keep ahead of the wave.

Rx to Resisting Change

Changing is scary, awkward, hard, uncomfortable, confusing and sometimes humiliating. How can we deal with change effectively and positively with such downsides?

Focus on the rewards of change. A comparable process would be exercise. Exercise can be painful, uncomfortable, make us feel inadequate, and sometimes humiliated at being out of shape. But those who stick with it experience benefits to exercise (see Chapter 10 – Power Move 1). That said, the challenges of exercise are overcome by focusing on the rewards. The same is true of change.

Make a list of the five benefits of change in your job. Take the time to be as detailed and thorough as possible as it relates to your specific job. In quiet and privacy, read this list and then say the statements below:

1. Change can be hard.
2. Change can be scary.
3. Change can be awkward.
4. Change can be confusing.
5. Change can be humiliating.
6. Change can be uncomfortable.
7. Change can be empowering.
8. I choose change.

4

MISTAKE 2
FEELING LIKE A VICTIM

It's tempting.

We tell our story. The more we tell it, the better we feel. Then we attract others with the similar stories. Done wrong. No control. Powerless. Not a clue into what was going on. Oh yes, there are the haves and the have nots. The dirty tricks. The biases. And finally, we never got a break.

Looking closer, though, we need to know the "victim" mentality paralyzes action, strength. It is a power move to avoid feeling sorry for yourself. But the victim mentality will not help you here. It simply wastes your time.

We need to tell a new story of success with "you" in control rather than about your loss caused by someone else. Accept the reality of your situation and then move on. Use the downsizing as a lever to become more resilient, add more value, and become even more productive.

Rx to Feeling Like a Victim

On paper, physically write a list of the five main wrongs done to you in this downsizing: the "victim" list. Now write a list of five empowerments you would like to feel in this situation.

1. Put the victim list in an envelope, seal it, and place it in your freezer. Yes, as silly as it sounds, "freeze it."

2. Place the list of your five wanted empowerments in your planner, briefcase, wallet, or purse. Keep this list with you at all times because I am going to ask you to refer to it often.

3. First thing each morning, read the good list aloud.

4. When you get to work, select a different item on the good list each day of the week to do something positive to make it come true. List it in your planner.

5. When you get home, read the good list aloud.

6. Before you go to sleep, read the good list aloud.

This process trains your brain to stop being a victim. You will not believe what "you" can actually do, all you can do. Your mind just needs a little programming.

By the way, I highly recommend keeping track of these readings daily. Keeping to this schedule will speed up your "victimless" recovery.

5

MISTAKE 3
PLAYING THE NEW GAME BY THE OLD RULES

Rather than continuing to play by the old rules, look closely at the new situation to determine what has changed. Then find out what the new priorities are and decide objectively what to focus on to best leverage your value. Play by the "new" rules and move yourself into the coming working model early. This gives you a better chance of keeping your job.

By the way, ignorance is no excuse. You are still judged by the new rules even when you don't know them One thing is for sure, in a downsizing there are definitely new rules. If you don't know what the new rules are, get yourself a mentor or coach. If this is not possible, ask questions of your manager or co-workers - get very curious.

The bottom line is this: find out what the new rules are and if they are ethical, moral, and doable, learn and follow them.

Rx to Playing by the New Rules

To play by the new rules you need to find out what they are. If you do not know what they are, do one of the following things:

- Acquire a mentor or coach or ask your manager or co-workers to share their view of the new rules with you. Meet often, more than once a month. Every other week, at a minimum, would be good.

- Simplify the rules in your mind and then write them in your planner to re-enforce them. Yes, you need a planner.

- List the reasons why the old rules do not work anymore below the listing of new rules.

- Read the new rules every morning before starting work to frame your actions for the day.

- Update the new rules often with continual input from your mentor, coach, friends and co-workers.

- If and when you feel like you want to use the old rules, read the new rules list again.

Play by the new rules every time. No exceptions. Change.

6

MISTAKE 4
TRYING TO CONTROL THE UNCONTROLLABLE

Is it practical to think we can really control this situation? You might be surprised how many think they can actually control a downsizing. This pointless struggle for control wastes precious time and effort. A more sensible strategy is to simply accept coming change completely and move forward.

... apply yourself 100% ...

By truly accepting the downsizing, you can apply yourself 100% to the new organization and focus on your options. You might imagine the frustration of trying to change the unchangeable. Not only is energy wasted, passion is diminished and hope is decimated.

An example of sensible action would be to first list all the things you have control over on a piece of paper. Next, list all the things that matter to you on the same piece of paper. What you work on should be the intersection of the two.

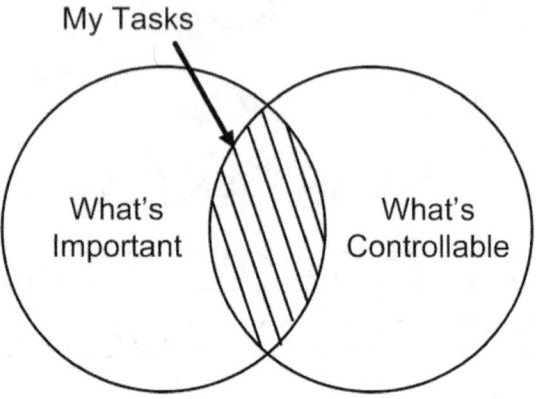

Rx to Stop Trying to Control the uncontrollable

To kick the habit of trying to control the uncontrollable, do the following.

1. In your planner, list five things in the downsizing you can control in your planner.

2. List five things in the downsizing you have absolutely no control over.

3. Read your "cannot control" list each morning at work five times. Accept you will not be able to control these things. Ask yourself to move on.

4. Read your "can control" list each morning at work five times. Note just one thing you can control in your planner each day. Control that.

7

MISTAKE 5
SLOWING DOWN

Whether you know it or not, you are probably being observed for value-add even before the downsizing is announced. As a result, slowing down will affect you in two ways. First, it will limit your positive exposure to those who make workforce reduction decisions. And second, it will dramatically reduce your opportunity to gain new skillsets that will make you attractive in the new organization.

So actually, speed up. Cover even more ground in your work. Give yourself the needed confidence to work much faster while maintaining your typical high quality. This gives you a better chance of an even higher evaluation.

Speeding up can cause anxiety for several reasons. You may feel more vulnerable with the possibility of making big mistakes. And mistakes, although management has formally stated are acceptable in the *New Working Model*, are not really acceptable.

Speeding up your work is the only course of action now. Deep down, you know this. But speeding up does not necessarily mean doing things faster. It does mean getting your work done faster. A good way to do work faster without speeding up tasks, is to practice advanced task management (Sanders, 2014). Work smarter with your existing task list.

Rx to Slowing Down

Speed up your work by practicing advanced task management techniques (refer to the Templates, Exercises, Systems chapter). Do the following:

1. List all your tasks (work and personal).
2. Perform MicroMeditation (see Templates, Exercises, Systems).
3. Prioritize all your tasks.
4. Validate task priorities with key stakeholders.
5. Create task queues (folders with key information).
6. Engage tasks (begin work on a task consulting your queue).
7. De-engage tasks (download all information before switching to another task).
8. Practice advanced task management (delete, delegate, transfer, reduce scope).
9. Get feedback from key stakeholders.
10. Act on this feedback
11. Repeat.

8

MISTAKE 6
PSYCHOLOGICALLY UNPLUGGING FROM YOUR JOB

It would be easy to just numb yourself to the downsizing and unplug from the job. That way you would not have to experience the painful, uncomfortable process of change. The only problem with this strategy is that unplugging only delays the inevitable. Sooner or later you have to face that freight train called "change."

Unplugging also puts you in a relatively weak position, unable to take advantage of opportunities that might be available to you during the downsizing process.

Instead, "fall in love" with your job. Keep the romance alive by focusing on the wonderful aspects of your job and then really enjoying them to the fullest.

Don't allow the stress of downsizing come between you and your beautiful work. Give yourself these two gifts: commitment and passion. Every day, before you get out of bed, say this: "Today I give myself the gifts of commitment and passion." Thank yourself.

Both qualities of commitment and passion will allow you to shine. Those in charge of the reduction-in-force will see you in your most positive light.

Rx to Plugging In to Your Job

In the evening, when it's quiet and you feel relaxed, make two lists. On the first, list the three things that hurt you or are unpleasant about your work on a piece of paper. Take time to reflect on this honestly. On the second, list three things that empower you about your work in your planner.

Put the list of job negatives in an envelope and place it in your freezer. This psychologically freezes the negative thinking that sticks to you daily. Take the second list of positives with you each day to and from work. Read the list three times daily – before work, at lunch, and when you get home. Incorporate ways to experience these three positive items into each workday.

MISTAKE 7
AVOIDING NEW ASSIGNMENTS

Now is not the time to shrink from work to see how things will eventually work out. It's not the time to become invisible. Instead, do just the opposite. Stretch yourself to take on new assignments to be better prepared for the future challenges ahead and add value.

Don't wait to be assigned new work. Instead, ask for new assignments. Broaden your experience and visibility to augment your organizational value. More experience and skills also make you more marketable if you are eventually separated as a result of the downsizing. There is no downside to taking on new work.

Avoiding assignments is a way to tune out and become invisible by playing a low-key role. This is a futile attempt to avoid the headache of change and possible mistakes. But this behavior only isolates you more and prevents management from seeing your strengths. Not a good strategy.

Instead, take on new assignments to show your motivation and willingness to get on board with the New Working Model and to showcase yourself for value add.

Rx to Avoiding New Assignments

Do the following to take on new assignments.

- List your tasks and priorities on paper and meet with your management to review. Get buy-in for your current workload and ask if you can do more.

- Watch what is going on around you and look for opportunities to cross-train and assist others in important tasks.

- Volunteer to be a liaison between your group and others to spearhead cross-functional initiatives. Here, it would be enough to simply set up meetings and facilitate task definitions, goals and schedules.

- Continually ping your co-workers and management about opportunities for growth and training.

- Continually ask your manager for opportunities for growth and new assignments. Here, ensure new assignments are related to the *New Working Model* and your position in the new organization.

Obtain a mentor or coach and ask for direction to take on more meaningful work. Note you can have more than one mentor.

10

EIGHT POWER MOVES
THRIVING IN CHAOS

In addition to avoiding or correcting the seven critical mistakes made in a downsizing, below are eight practical steps you can take to help you reduce stress and focus. Stress and lack of focus can be debilitating when dealing with the continual challenges of significant change. These steps, or power moves, include:

1. Exercising
2. Drinking more water
3. Having fun, smiling and laughing
4. Getting plenty of sleep
5. Being grateful
6. Saying nice things to yourself
7. Simplifying your life
8. Forgiving and forgetting

Power Move 1 - Exercise

Exercise three times a week. With doctor approval, a workout for even for 15-30 minutes a day, three times a week does wonders to reduce stress. Whether it's a brisk walk, a workout at the gym, or doing a few sit-ups in your living room, get your body moving. Exercise helps your body function better and sets you up for a good attitude, a crisp mind, and better overall health. It also helps you digest your food and sleep better.

One exercise regimen you might consider is the Five Tibetan Rites. This set of five body movements is a mix of Yoga and light abdominal and leg exercises. You can find them on the internet or email me for a link.

Power Move 2 - Drink More Water

Drink a lot more water. Most of us do not drink enough water. Water is absolutely necessary for your body to function properly as well as detox on a daily basis. Your brain is composed of over 70% water. So consider drinking an ample supply of water, watering your brain.

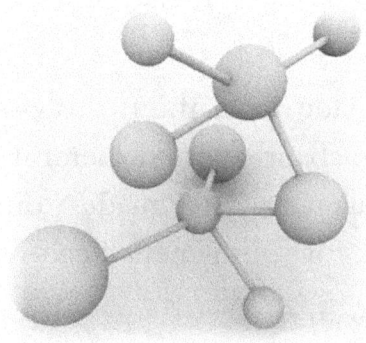

How much water should we drink? Divide your weight in pounds by two – that's how many ounces of water you should drink every day.

For instance, if you weigh 160 pounds, your daily water quota would be 160 divided by 2, or 80 ounces of water. Since there are 128 ounces of water in one gallon, 80 ounces would be about two thirds of a gallon, or about 2 & 1/2 quarts (32 ounces per quart).

Note: *Doctors recommend drinking eight, eight-ounce glasses of water per day. This amounts to 64 ounces. However, using our formula, this amount would be appropriate for someone with weighing about 130 pounds or less.*

Do the math for yourself and drink at least your quota each day. Please note that tea, coffee, alcohol, and juices are not substitutes for water. And know that alcohol is a dehydrator. This explains why you may get a headache from a hangover – your brain is relatively dry and it hurts!

So if you drink alcohol, drink twice the amount of recommended water to combat dehydration. Drinking more water also helps you maintain your ability to do critical thinking and stave off a hangover.

Additionally, drink high quality water. There are many types of water to choose from. Choices include bottled water, home-filtered tap water, reverse osmosis, mineral enhanced, and hydrolyzed water.

I recommend drinking water made from the hydrolysis process. Hydrolyzed water is more absorbent and therefore hydrates your body better. And alkaline water made from hydrolysis is also considered better for your general health.

The bottom line: drink a lot of water.

Power Move 3 - Have Fun, Smile, Laugh

Humor is wonderful medicine for stress. Laugh at yourself more often and bring your light heart onto the workplace. You will become a delightful counterbalance to potentially depressing attitudes and dark work environment. Laughter and having a bit of fun also promotes good health and makes you look younger.

Smile! Smile at your co-workers – even if you don't know them. You'll be surprised when they smile back! This can be a lot of fun and raise morale at the same time. Make sure you know when you are smiling by practicing in a mirror. Then smile away. By the way, when you smile, it makes you happy as well.

Power Move 4 - Get Plenty of Sleep

Restlessness and late-night preoccupations can result in poor sleep patterns, especially during stressful situations. Be aware of the effects of lack of sleep and benefits of adequate sleep. Seven to eight hours a night are recommended. But we are all different. If you are having trouble sleeping, try taking a shower, a short walk, or reading a book before bedtime. Avoid late-night eating, alcohol, or caffeine.

Power Move 5 - Be Grateful, Thankful

It's easy to obsess on what we don't have. Try appreciating what you do have: education, skills, health, family, friends, and safety. Think about those without most of these gifts and realize your life is pretty good. And think about your bright future in the long run. Picture yourself successful and happy in your job instead of the doom of unemployment. Count on this and be grateful in advance. A positive attitude can move mountains.

Power Move 6 - Say Nice Things to You

Thoughts may naturally drift negative, critical. Avoid this. There are good reasons why you made it to where you are today. Remember and hold onto these as you begin your new journey. You can become your own best friend by treating yourself well. I guarantee you will appreciate it!

Power Move 7 - Simplify Your Life

In times of stress, it's important to get back to basics. A complex lifestyle can become overwhelming and affect your relationships at work and at home, not to mention your work performance. Simplify. This will allow you to do less extremely well rather than a lot poorly.

Power Move 8 - Forgive, Forget

Grudges have no upside. Forgiveness is a wonderful antidote to the pain and stress caused from potential job loss. If you are having difficulty forgiving those you think have wronged you, try something seemingly wacky – do something nice for them. Amazingly, this works. With the burden of the grudge lifted, you can focus on your work at hand: Operation Ride the Wave!

Rx to Deal with Chaos

To deal effectively with the chaotic nature of a downsizing, it is important to practice all eight Power Moves consistently and continually. To accomplish this, do the following:

1. List Power Moves 1 through 7 in your planner.
2. Focus on one Power Move each day of the week – your choice.
3. Touch all seven Power Moves at least once a week.
4. Practice Power Move 8 every day: forgive, forget.

11

SURVIVAL SYNDROME
ENTER THE NEW WORKING MODEL

If you have survived a recent downsizing, many issues remain. These issues may prevent you from both excelling and being happy with your job. The New Working Model may now be causing you to question your good fortune. You may feel you are on shaky ground, having a myriad of emotions  and simply not enjoying your work anymore. Below is a description of ten after effects of downsizing and what you can do about them.

This "after downsizing" condition is commonly referred to as the "Survivors' Syndrome."

After the reduction-in-force was announced at your company, you may have worried and then quickly tried to position yourself well to save your job. Then the fateful day came and your friends and associates received their news, one at a time. They were either be retained, moved or let go.

Of those who were severed, some were terminated immediately while others were let go with notice. But for those with notice, to keep their handsome severance packages they had to play nice. These downsized would have to transfer critical knowledge as well as help those retained set up the *New Working Model*. These were phantoms with faces – the walking terminated.

But enough of that. "You" made it! You were retained, one of the lucky ones. What a relief! At least for a little while. Then the "Syndrome" begins to kick in. You start to question who really won.

Guilt

You may feel guilt. After all, why were you spared and not others? They were just as qualified. Some who were let go were even more qualified. Why me? And what will happen to the families of those downsized, their well-being? And the stigma of being laid off may follow these past co-workers to their new job interviews, hampering them in getting a new job.

Mistrust

You may lack trust in your post-downsizing management. Were there strings attached and favors pulled for some of those retained? You may not understand the logic of some of the retentions and separations. They didn't make any sense. Was this fair? And does it bode poorly of your own future in a seemingly unfair organization? Can you trust this new management?

Concern

You may become increasingly concerned about your ability to perform. You are now being asked to do "less with less." But after a short time, you realize this actually means "more with less." This was never more clear because your clients were never informed of the "less" part by your management. Your clients still expect the same service level, if not more.

As a result, you need to do much more, much faster and your work quality may suffer as a result. You may now be judged to impossible standards. So you ask yourself, "Is this job even doable?" You are now concerned about your future in an organization where you may not be able to perform well. You're in jeopardy.

The Malfunctioning Working Model

You may realize you are knee-deep in a "poorly working" *New Working Model*. This is because many of the simplest processes and tasks just aren't working well anymore. What did management expect? The *New Working Model* was created in "secrecy" without your organization's subject-matter-experts to ensure the details of the downsizing were kept confidential. But this new model is flawed, both in process fluidity, handoffs, role mapping, and accountability. There are now gaps and overlaps in the model's work flows. This is not only creating considerable conflict with role confusion and finger pointing, but key important processes are now beginning to fail. You're losing confidence in the new organization.

Sadness

You begin to miss your co-workers who were let go. Your routine has changed. The workplace is just not the same anymore. It's actually become quite depressing. You find yourself walking by your old co-workers' offices, remembering the good times before the reductions. You realize you don't enjoy coming to work as much and have to force yourself to have a positive attitude. You feel sad.

Anxiety

You are continually feeling anxiety. Your management was secretive about the downsizing and you fear another one may be in the works. Any potential sign of future reductions becomes real evidence to you of another impending layoff. As a result, you are having trouble concentrating on your job and trusting management. After all, the last reduction was done in secret. They may be planning another. It has become more and more difficult to motivate yourself to work hard. You think, "Why put in the extra effort when it may all be for nothing?"

Distracted from Work, Looking Elsewhere

You may now find yourself looking for opportunities outside the company. Your job seems to be getting harder and riskier; in some cases, it seems nearly impossible to perform well. Due to the faster pace, mistakes and failures are not only possible, they are becoming common. This makes you extremely uncomfortable.

Your management has formally communicated to the workforce that mistakes and failures are acceptable. They say mistakes are even expected in the *New Working Model* and considered learning opportunities. But you feel in your heart, "not really."

You believe deep down inside that mistakes will label you as a poor performer and could hurt your job performance evaluation going forward.

Perceived Pay Cut

You may feel like you're actually taking a pay cut. The company may have raised its performance evaluation bar for annual reviews and, if available, may be downgrading profit sharing plans. Benefits seem to be decreasing in value and the employee co-pays may be increasing. And if you calculate the additional hours you may be putting in now, your net hourly rate may be significantly less after the downsizing. Work-life balance is shifting.

Less Flexible Work Hours

Your pre-downsized flexible working hours may have become less flexible under the New Working Model as individual performance is now under greater scrutiny. In response, employee competition may be increasing causing co-workers to come into work earlier and leaving work later. Also, due to less employee availability, you may also be increasingly called into meetings late in workdays or even after-hours or weekends.

Conflicts and Disagreements

You may now be experiencing more conflicts and disagreements with your co-workers. This may be the result of the New Working Model's poor role definition, lack of personal accountability, dysfunctional procedures and processes, missed hand-offs, and inadequate knowledge transfer. Employees, not wanting to take blame for the dysfunctional model, may feel they need to assign blame to co-workers.

Another reason for conflict and disagreements may be a heightened competitiveness between co-workers. This could be the result of employees continuing to position themselves for perceived promotional opportunities in the New Working Model or from a fear of even more lay-offs in the months to come.

Unhealthy employee-employee culture can be debilitating and destructive, resulting in evolving polarization and damage to both teaming activities and cross-functional collaboration. The culture may be becoming more abrasive and impersonal.

Rx to Survive the New Working Model

Spend some alone time with yourself periodically to build and rebuild your energy. Make appointments with yourself one weekend day a month, an evening during the week, a lunch hour, a vacation day, whenever - and be alone. Unplug, leaving your smartphone, pager, laptop at home, in the car, on the desk, at the office, where-ever.

Once alone, there may be anxiety at first. It won't last. Say out loud the following, starting and ending your alone time:

1. I have nothing to feel guilty about, it is not my fault.
2. I choose to trust, giving the benefit of the doubt.
3. I have little to be concerned about, it will work out.
4. I accept my sadness and allow it to go through me.
5. I have little to feel anxiety about, it will all work out.
6. I want to look for other work, but not desperately.
7. I will focus on my work that I love.
8. I make a good salary and have great benefits.
9. I will be flexible in changing times.
10. Conflicts, disagreements are necessary for growth.

Again, do this when you start. And again before you finish your alone time. I recommend spending at least an hour. But your ultimate goal would be to give yourself a complete day. You will love this gift to you. I guarantee it. Take a selfie!

12

CHALLENGING THE NEW WORKING MODEL

BECOMING SELF CONTAINED

Throughout the downsizing and its aftermath, you kept saying just one thing to yourself, "At least I still have a job." But somehow, this just isn't not good enough anymore. What you need is a few tips to survive your own survival! Below are ten suggestions to overcome the deficiencies of the *New Working Model* and survive the Survivor's Syndrome challenges discussed in Chapter 11.

But our goal is to do more than just survive, it is to thrive after a downsizing. So above using the antidotes to the seven critical mistakes described in Chapters 2-8 and the Power Moves described in Chapter 9, add the additional steps below to deal with Survivors' Syndrome and contain the *New Working Model*.

Practice Intensive Task Management

The fact is you have more on your plate than you can possibly do. As a result, you need to practice task management to reduce your workload. Reducing your task load will allow you to do your work better, with higher quality. Task management involves deleting tasks, delegating tasks, transferring tasks, and reducing task scope. Mastering task management may require developing new skills such as conflict management, negotiation, delegation, project scope management, and interpersonal communications.

Post-downsizing survival will require covering even more ground in your work while maintaining your typical high quality. Do this by relentlessly managing your task load. Reduce your tasks and task complexity to make more time to complete your workload with ease and high quality with proper work-life balance.

Fall in Love with Your Work, Again

Consider the Bob Dylan song, "Things have changed." You need to take advantage of change, all the new opportunities now available to you during and after the downsizing. In pressing forward, fall back in love with your job by focusing on the wonderful aspects of your work while looking for opportunities to realize them within the changes.

This may mean you will need work a few more hours to do the extra required to take on the extra work you are good at and love - the work that makes you shine. Most managers will never reject your appeal to do more. Not only will you fall in love with your work, you'll do more networking within the company and strengthen your skills at the same time.

Another thing you can do is teach. Suggest a brown-bag lecture series or volunteer to coach and mentor through company-sponsored programs. This will not only allow you to sharpen your communication skills and brush up on skills, you will distinguish yourself as a leader and subject matter expert.

Expand Your Business Affiliations

It's a good idea to either expand or initiate business affiliations. Business affiliations allow you to network, gain experience and knowledge, learn new skillsets, earn certifications, and find mentors and coaches. These affiliations can be through business, alumni or charity associations. As you re-enter or join, get involved. Volunteer to assist the group by being on a committee, joining a team, or accepting a management role.

You may also try speaking at events on a topic of your expertise or interest to again establish yourself as a subject matter expert.

Continue Your Education

More education can only help you in the workplace. Your degree, if more than ten years old, needs a refresh. And if you do not have one, it's time to complete your degree. Many employers have educational re-imbursement. Try to use all of it every year!

If you would like to get a certification or take a course not covered by your company's educational reimbursement program, make a business case for it and propose your company pay for it out of its training budget. A business case is important because it will help your management sell the training to higher level managers and executives.

Understand a business case does not need to be complicated. It need only contain a detailed description of the certification/course, its timing, how the training relates to your work, how it can be helpful to others on the job, and what it costs. You might also want to add the reputation of the institution and the general value of the certification or course.

There also may be many courses offered at work on topics of interest and relevance to your work. Take all the courses you can make time for. More education helps you get smarter, better skilled, more networked, and exercises your brain. It also makes you more marketable in your current position and outside the company. Again, there is no down side to this approach.

Become Your Own Hero

Re-invent yourself. Ultimately, surviving in the new organization will require you to re-invent yourself. To do this, become your own hero, your own role model. Learn to have fun, don't be afraid to laugh.

Humor is wonderful medicine for stress. Laugh at yourself more often and bring your light heart onto the workplace. You will become a delightful counterbalance to potentially depressing attitudes and a dark work environment. Laughter and fun also promotes better health and makes you look younger. It may also be viewed by your management as a valuable asset in challenging times.

Keep in Touch with Laid-off Work Friends

You may feel angry, hurt, sad or guilty regarding co-workers who were let go in the downsizing. Deal with these feelings by keeping in touch with your old friends. Set up a luncheon or after work meeting. Invite current employees as well. You may be shocked! Many times these past employees are doing better than you are.

For one thing, your old work friends are probably getting much-needed rest. They may even look healthier. The stress of their work and the downsizing gone now, they may even look a bit younger. Some go on to get better jobs, either in pay, location or work type. Others may decide to travel while others may have gone back to school. You'll find as many personal stories as there are people.

The point is your world stayed the same and their worlds have changed. Meeting up with these past co-workers will go a long way to relieve much of the anger, hurt, sadness and guilt you may be feeling. And it will go a long way to allow proper closure to enable you to move on.

If feelings of anger, hurt, sadness or guilt persist, get help. Your company most likely has an employee assistance program of some kind. Take advantage of counseling to deal with your feelings. There is nothing wrong with having feelings and certainly nothing to be ashamed of to ask for help. Recommend this to your co-workers who have the same feelings as well.

Train your Mind for Happiness

As we read in Power Move 5, be truly grateful and thankful for what you have and what you've accomplished. It's so easy to obsess on what we do not have or what we have not done. Try appreciating what you do have: your family, friends, health and safety. Marvel at all you have done, your skills, experience, education, and job!

When you think about all you have, you can see your life is actually pretty wonderful. If you do this work in perspective, when negative thoughts come, you will have the ammunition to turn them back into positive thoughts. Picture yourself successful and happy in your re-invented job. A positive attitude can move mountains.

Also realize, however tempting, grudges have only a downside. They cause you to defocus and divert you from the important work and relationship building at hand. Grudges can arise from the loss of co-workers, loss of your simpler pre-downsizing life, and loss of the feeling of job security. It is easy to blame. But blame is essentially a prison of thought with nothing productive to be had.

Forgiveness is the perfect antidote to grudges. But if you find it difficult to forgive, try doing something nice for that person or organization. This actually works! Letting go of grudges is the only real way to let go of the past and focus on your new work, your new self.

Refuse to play the role of the victim in a downsizing. You are much bigger than this. Instead, take charge of the events in your life, your job, your career. Find out what matters to you and what you can control in the workplace. Work with that. Do more than just survive. **Win.**

Rx to Challenging the New Working Model

The prescription to meet the challenge of the *New Working Model* is to simply be one yourself. That is, change.

This means doing more things, different things, and challenging things and doing these things before they become critically necessary. That is, if you wait that long, it's too late.

Practice one of the seven self-containing tools each day of the week to challenge the *New Working Model*.

Monday practice task management, Tuesday love your work, Wednesday develop business affiliations, Thursday look into more education, Friday become your own hero, Saturday get in touch with old friends let go from the job, and Sunday train your brain for happiness.

TEMPLATES, EXERCISES, SYSTEMS

This appendix provides helpful templates, exercises, and systems referred to within this book.

- Action Plan Template
- MicroMeditation Exercise
- Attention Focusing Exercise
- Week at a Glance Planner System
- Advanced Task Management System

Action Plan Template

The Action Plan can be an effective one-page tool to get significant tasks under control and managed well.

Task Goal and Sponsor/Client

Task Scope of Work

Task Team

Subtasks & Actions (30 Days)			
Subtask/Action	Due	Name	Status

Issues (Resolutions) & Risks (Mitigations)
Issue: _____. Resolution: _____
Risk: _____. Mitigation: _____

Notes & Reference information

©2010-14 Mike Sanders

MicroMeditation Exercise

Another way to access our prefrontal cortex (or higher brain) for higher level thinking and planning is to perform visualization. When visualizing, you are squarely accessing your prefrontal cortex. MicroMeditation is a good way to perform visualization in a very short time – just 60 seconds! The six steps below are done in 10-second increments ending with your answer to a very important question, "what do you want?" The key is to answer this important question in just one or two words. Follow the steps below (ten seconds each):

1. Breathe in, exhale.
2. Breathe in, exhale.
3. Breathe in, visualize a banana.
4. Breathe in, peel the banana.
5. Breathe in, take a bite of the banana.
6. Breathe and answer "What do you want?"

Everything you do on your task list should fall under and be consistent with your answer to the question, "what you want." Use this prior to and for task prioritization.

Attention Focusing Exercise

The attention focusing exercise helps you pull yourself back into the task at hand or to simply clear your mind of negative unproductive thinking. I recommend at least twice per day, between 5 to 50 repetitions. Done frequently, you will train you brain to focus and defocus at will. This ability can be critical when you absolutely have to be focused.

1. Breathe in, count 1, Exhale, count 1
2. Breathe in, count 2, Exhale, count 2
3. Breathe in, count 3, Exhale, count 3
4. Breathe in, count 4, Exhale, count 4
5. Breathe in, count 5, Exhale, count 5
6. Repeat

This exercise works in almost any situation and for any period of time as well as repetition. That is, some benefit can come from the smallest of time doing it.

As you do the exercise, clear your mind and notice what pulls your thoughts away. Then gently pull yourself back into the exercise and continue.

As you notice particular recurring distractions, they will eventually go away, allowing you to focus much better on the task at hand. This exercise has the additional benefit of peace of mind.

Week at a Glance Planner System

Below is a template of a personal planner. The view is a week at a glance. The left page is for notes. The right page is for weekly tasks.

Planner Template

For more information on the week-at-a-glance planner system, refer to the book, Advanced Multitasking: Do More Work Less, Be Happy (Sanders, 2014). The book is available on Amazon.com.

Planner Sample

Advanced Task Management System

The Advanced Multitasking™ task management process is shown below. The process includes cognitive thinking listing all tasks, task prioritization, priority validation, creating task queues, task engagement/de-engagement, and task reduction management.

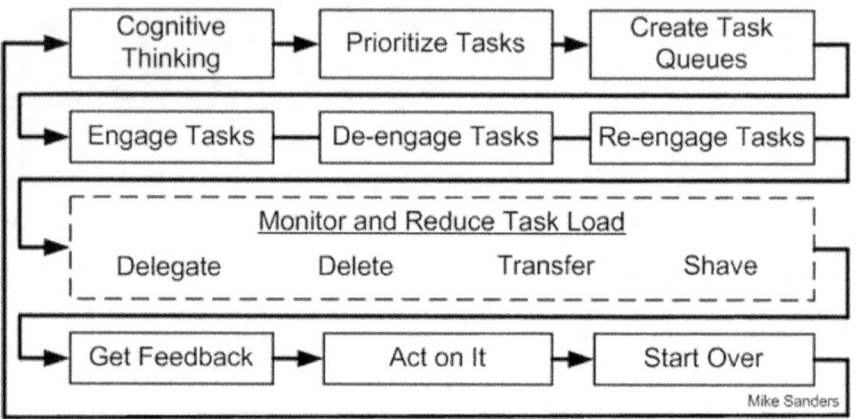

Advanced Multitasking Model

For more information on advanced task management, refer to the book, Advanced Multitasking: Do More Work Less, Be Happy (Sanders, 2014), available on Amazon.com.

Free file and template downloads are available at Advanced-Multitasking.com.

REFERENCES AND SUGGESTED READING

Astrachan, J. (1995). Organizational departures: The impact of separation anxiety as studied in a mergers and acquisitions simulation. *Journal of Applied Behavioral Science, 31*(1), 31-50.

Baruch, B, & Hing, P. (1997). Survivor's syndrome – a management myth?' *Journal of Managerial Psychology. 15*(1), 29-45.

Berglas, S. (2009, February 11). Dealing with survivor syndrome. *Forbes.* Retrieved from http://www.forbes.com/2009/02/11/survivor-syndrome-recession-entrepreneurs-manage_0211_survivor.html

Boatright, J. (2009). *Ethics and the conduct of business (6th ed.).* Upper Saddle River, NJ: Prentice Hall.

Brockner, J. (1992). Managing the effects of layoffs on survivors. *California Management Review, 34*(2), 9-28.

Carbery, R., & Garavan, T. (2005). Organisational restructuring and downsizing: Issues related to learning, training and employability of survivors. *Journal of European Industrial Training, 29*(6), 488-522.

Casteneda, C. (1968). *The teachings of Don Juan: A Yaqui way of knowledge.* Berkeley, CA: University of California Press.

Cohen, D. (2004). *The one who is not busy: Connecting with work in a satisfying way.* New York, NY: Gibbs-Smith.

Comaford, C. (2012, April 4). Got inner peace? 5 ways to get it now. *Forbes.com.* Retrieved from http://www.forbes.com/sites/christinecomaford/2012/04/04/got-inner-peace-5-ways-to-get-it-now/

Dvorsky, G. (2007, March 19). Managing your 50,000 daily thoughts. *SentientThoughts.com.* Retrieved from http://www.sentientdevelopments.com/2007/03/managing-your-50000-daily-thoughts.html

Galbraith, J. K. (2004). Downsizing in America: Reality, causes, & consequences. *The American Prospect, 15,* 69-70.

Garvin, D., Edmondson, A., & Gino, F. (2008). Is yours a learning organization? *Harvard Business Review.* Retrieved from http://hbr.org/2008/03/is-yours-a-learning-organization/ar/1

Gown, J. (2010, October 15). Why your brain needs water. *Psychology Today.* Retrieved from http://www.psychologytoday.com/blog/you-illuminated/201010/why-your-brain-needs-water

Hawthorne, J. (2009). Change your thoughts, change your world. *Jennifer Read Hawthorne.* Retrieved from http://www.jenniferhawthorne.com/articles/change_your_thoughts.html

Johnson, S. (2002). *Who moved my cheese?* New York, NY: Putnam.

Kittredge, G. L. (1939). *The tragedy of Hamlet, prince of Denmark by William Shakespeare*. Boston, MA: Ginn and Company.

Macky, K. (2004). Organisational downsizing and redundancies: The New Zealand workers' experience. *New Zealand Journal of Employment Relations, 29*(1), 63-87.

Nycz-Conner, J. (2009, January 26). Survivor syndrome. *Washington Business Journal.* Retrieved from http://www.bizjournals.com/washington/stories/2009/01/26/smallb2.html?page=all

Popkin, B. M., D'Anci, K. E. & Rosenberg, I. H. (2010, August). Water, hydration, and health. *US National Library of Sciences.* Retrieved from http://www.ncbi.nlm.nih.gov/pmc/articles/PMC2908954/

Rigby, D. (2002). *Look before you lay off.* Harvard Business Review, 80, 20-21.

Sanders, M. (2014). *Advanced Multitasking.* Los Angeles, CA: Create Space.

Smeltzer, L., & Zener, F. (1994). Minimizing the negative effect of employee layoffs through effective announcements. *Employee Counseling Today, 6*(4), 3-3.

Tolle, E. (1999). *The power* of *now*. Novato, CA: Namaste Publishing.

This page intentionally left blank.

SEMINARS

7 Critical Mistakes Employees Make in a Downsizing

Controlling Communication Channels

Beyond Emotional Intelligence

Rise of the Knowledge Worker

Downsizing Survival Kit

Advanced Multitasking

Power Networking

SuperConnectivity

Business Writing

Mike has spoken at over 150 business and corporate events throughout California and Nevada. Venues include business associations, conferences and symposiums, universities, corporations, and governments.

Email or call if you are interested in these management presentations at your event, company or organization.

mike@mike-sanders.com - 714-615-5477

LinkedIn: www.linkedin.com/in/mikesanders1

FREE DOWNLOADS

www.advanced-multitasking.com

Five Tibetan Rites Exercise

SuperBrain Yoga Exercise

Action Plan Template

Stress Reduction Kit

Engagement Templates

Email Mike for passwords at mike@mike-sanders.com

www.ingramcontent.com/pod-product-compliance
Lightning Source LLC
Chambersburg PA
CBHW071806170526
45167CB00003B/1192